MW01705874

REBEL GIRLS SPORT

A'JA WILSON

THE BEST IS YET TO COME

In collaboration with

Copyright © 2025 by Rebel Girls, Inc.

Rebel Girls supports copyright. Copyright fuels creativity, encourages diverse voices, promotes free speech, and creates a vibrant culture. Thank you for enjoying an authorized edition of this book and for complying with copyright laws by not reproducing, scanning, or distributing any part of it in any form without permission. You are supporting indie creators as well as allowing Rebel Girls to publish books for Rebel Girls, wherever they may be.

NIKE and the Swoosh design are owned, registered, and licensed by NIKE.

Good Night Stories for Rebel Girls and Rebel Girls are registered trademarks.

Rebel Girls, Inc.
421 Elm Ave.
Larkspur, CA 94939
www.rebelgirls.com

Text by Sarah Parvis
Illustrations by Monet Alyssa
Designed by Georgia Rucker

PHOTO CREDITS: 3: Nell Redmond/AP Images. 6–9: Courtesy A'ja Wilson. 10: © ESPN. 11: Tony Gutierrez/AP Images. 12: Courtesy A'ja Wilson. 13: Sipa USA via AP Images. 14: Nike. 17: Erica Denhoff/Icon Sportswire ECS/Newscom. 20: Harry How/Getty Images. 25: DeeCee Carter/MediaPunch/IPX via AP Images. 28–31: Nike. 32–33: Rebel Girls.

SPECIAL THANKS: Amy Pfister, Anjelika Temple, Annie Liu, Denise Gomez-Rivera, Erika Harvey, Haley Dapkus, Isadora Manzaro, Jes Wolfe, Joy Smith, Michon Vanderpoel, Rachel Toby

Printed in Canada, 2025
10 9 8 7 6 5 4 3 2 1

ISBN: 979-8-88964-161-2

MIX
Paper | Supporting responsible forestry
FSC™ C018179
FSC www.fsc.org

CONTENTS

HI REBELS,

I have spent most of my life on a basketball court. I'm a player, a coach, and a fan. I spent eight years in the WNBA. I've won three Olympic golds as a player and one as a coach. So I know something about the game. And I know something about what it takes to play at the highest levels of the game.

I couldn't have been happier when A'ja decided to come to South Carolina. Because she is crazy good. She is funny, she is smart, and she is an **amazing teammate**. On top of all of that, she has an insatiable desire to be great. And that fire has made her an **absolute legend**.

In basketball, we often think of a player as legendary for what they do on the court. The magic of A'ja is all the other stuff. She has touched so many lives—not just in our community or in South Carolina, but nationally and internationally. Hers is a story that is not often written, and I am beyond proud to celebrate her for the ways she has displayed her talent and her voice.

Simply put: **Our world is better because A'ja Wilson is in it.**

Think of all she has accomplished. She is a two-time WNBA champ, a three-time WNBA MVP, and a six-time WNBA All-Star. She's a best-selling author and an incredible role model. She's accomplished everything she has set out to do—and she's 28 years old. She has so much more to offer the sport of basketball and the world at large.

To the young people reading this book: I hope you enjoy A'ja's story, and I hope you are inspired by her talent, her focus, and the joy she brings to the game to go out there and be your best you too.

—DAWN STALEY, head coach, University of South Carolina

NIKE
NIKE
22

A'JA'S STORY

FROM UNDECIDED TO UNSTOPPABLE

FINDING HER PASSION

It was Saturday morning in Hopkins, South Carolina, and A'ja was fast asleep. Suddenly, her father's booming voice echoed across her brain.

"Time to get up," he said. "Time to get to the gym."

"Daaaaad," she groaned, throwing the covers over her head. "It's early."

He didn't budge.

Uh-oh, he's serious, she realized and dragged herself out of bed.

The future three-time MVP did not want to spend her day sweating through drills with her dad. But her father was adamant, so off she went.

A former player himself, he truly loved the game. He knew how to spot talent, and he saw it in A'ja.

But A'ja wasn't sold on basketball. Not yet anyway.

Her journey to the hoop took a bunch of twists and turns. A'ja played the piano and tried out tap dancing and ballet. She explored soccer, track, swimming, and even tennis. However, it was volleyball that truly unlocked her passion for sports. In fact, A'ja says volleyball was her first love. She was a swift passer and an impressive blocker. Her teammates would send high passes her way, and she'd attack with her powerful left hand. Mostly, she got to have fun!

FIERCE FACT

Playing volleyball taught A'ja skills that she uses to play strong defense to this day. She says she learned how to quick-jump, how to time her jumps right, and how to contest shots without fouling.

FINDING HER FOOTING

At about 10 years old, A'ja decided to give basketball a shot. She joined a coed rec league and became the only girl on a team full of boys who were reluctant to pass her the ball.

One day, in the middle of a game, the ball flew toward her. She scooped it up and scanned the court. With no one between her and the hoop, she took off. She felt invincible as she flew past the other players and launched into a layup. Midair, she realized something was wrong.

She was shooting on the wrong hoop!

She felt embarrassed and defeated, so she left that gym and took a long break from basketball. But A'ja has always been curious and resilient. And after three years, she was ready to try again. This time, basketball lit a fire inside her. She wanted to be good. No, scratch that. She wanted to be GREAT.

"I LEARNED AT A YOUNG AGE THAT I COULD PUSH MY LIMITS AND BE UNCOMFORTABLE."

Her dad bought her a hoop, and her mom stationed her outside by two big flowerpots. "These are your defenders," she said. And A'ja was on them. You could not pull her away.

Day or night, she was out there with the flowerpots and her hoop. If it was raining, she was outside practicing her shot. If the sun was scorching, she was out there, bounding from one side of her small court to the other. Even if it was snowing! Okay, it didn't ever snow in Hopkins, South Carolina. But if it did, A'ja would be there in her mittens, working on her layups.

A'JA'S STORY

PUTTING IN THE WORK

A'ja joined recreation leagues, and later, her father and a friend started a teen travel team. At first, A'ja spent all her time on the bench. She was happy to cheer for her teammates, but she eventually wanted to do more. She wanted to shine.

A'ja and her father got to work.

"My dad made sure that I had the fundamentals in my back pocket," said A'ja. "It wasn't just, 'All right, go out there and start shooting threes and see how many you can make.'" Instead, they trained. Day after day, she did Mikan drills, where she practiced shooting a layup with her right hand, then catching the ball and going directly for a layup with her left hand. It tested her coordination, her rhythm, her rebound skills, her stamina, and her determination to get better.

When they weren't on the court, A'ja was studying games. She and her dad would go to college games together to scrutinize the players' strategies and skills.

FIERCE FACT

When she hit her growth spurt, A'ja asked Coach Dad to push her even harder. Soon, she was staying after practice to run extra drills while wearing a weighted vest and using a five-pound ball.

THE MAKING OF A'STAR

The training wasn't easy. A'ja and her dad would push hard in practice during the day. And then, lying in bed at night, A'ja would run through moves in her head, mentally honing her skills. She'd picture her shots and focus on her follow-through, making sure it was crisp and clean. And the next day? She'd get up and hustle some more.

A'ja's dedication paid off. Her game improved, and she felt fierce. All the while, her father had her back, encouraging her to find her rhythm and tap into her greatness.

As a high school senior, A'ja was racking up 35 points and 15 rebounds per game—and scoring awesome accolades while she was at it. She was named a Parade All-American and crowned the 2014 National High School Player of the Year. Top college teams were courting the six-foot-five dynamo. Giant bins of letters from colleges overflowed in her living room.

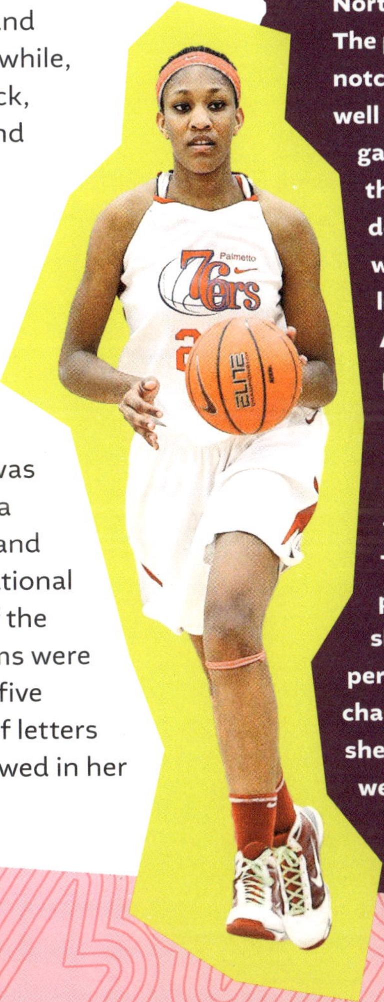

STATE CHAMPS

Going into her senior year of high school, A'ja had her eyes on an exciting prize: winning the state championship. It was A'ja and her team from Heathwood Hall versus Northwood Academy. The players were top-notch, the teams were well matched, and the game was an absolute thriller. Heathwood was down by three points with seven seconds left in the game when A'ja sank a three-pointer to force the game into overtime. At the final buzzer, Heathwood took the top honor, 66–58. Though 37 of those points were A'ja's, she insisted, "One person can't win a championship." Beaming, she said, "My teammates were amazing."

A'JA'S STORY

THERE'S NO PLACE LIKE HOME

A'ja was ranked the number one high school prospect, and college basketball fans nationwide couldn't wait to find out what jersey she'd wear. When it came time for A'ja to announce her decision, she made sure ESPN sent a camera crew—just like they did for the top male prospects. "I wanted all the little girls out there who love basketball to be flipping channels and say, 'Oh. I see you,'" she said.

Her high school gym was jam-packed with friends, family, fans, and members of the media when A'ja leaned in to the microphone and said, "There's no place like home."

She'd chosen to stay in her beloved home state and play for the University of South Carolina!

A POWERFUL PAIR

As A'ja made the transition from high school to college, coach Dawn Staley mentored her and gave her unforgettable advice. She explained to A'ja that there would be other talented athletes on the court. "They'll be quicker, stronger, faster, whatever, but they're not you," she said. "They can't do the things that you do."

Dawn pushed A'ja to be her best. She even benched A'ja during her freshman year. But they both agree it was worth it. A'ja studied her new team, unlocked her confidence, and, a few months later, was named Freshman of the Year.

COLLEGE LEGEND

Trusting the expert direction of coach Dawn Staley, A'ja honed her talents. With her height and power, she relentlessly blocked shots. With her speed and precision, she dominated close to the basket and rocked it with free throws. With her good nature and competitive spirit, she energized her teammates and led the Gamecocks to victory in the Southeastern Conference (SEC) four years in a row.

A'ja rose to meet any challenges that came her way. When the pressure of being in the spotlight felt overwhelming or when she had to deal with anxiety or an ankle injury, she leaned into her values and, with the support of her coach, teammates, and community, she persevered.

Under her leadership, South Carolina won its first NCAA tournament championship in 2017. A'ja broke countless school records, was named the SEC Player of the Year three times, and graduated as USC's all-time leader in points (2,389) and blocks (363).

FIERCE FACT

A'ja's college career was so legendary that the university commissioned an 11-foot-tall bronze statue of her. She's the first woman to get her own statue on campus.

"I WOULDN'T TRADE IN ANYTHING FOR THE TIME I'VE HAD AT SOUTH CAROLINA."

A'JA'S STORY

AN ACE ON THE COURT

As A'ja's chart-topping years as a Gamecock came to a close, it was time for her to rise to her next challenge: the WNBA. The top draft pick of 2018, she was snapped up by the Las Vegas Aces. Soon, she was mixing it up on the court and proving her power. Hard to guard and a confident shot from all angles, she earned the Rookie of the Year trophy. And she followed that up with three MVP awards. With her bold play and motivating leadership, she ushered the Aces to back-to-back championships.

On September 15, 2024, with two minutes left on the clock in a matchup with the Connecticut Sun, A'ja broke a new record, becoming the first WNBA player to score 1,000 points in a single season. And even as she celebrated, she shared her triumph. "My teammates are the heartbeat," she said, beaming. "They keep me going. I don't get any points without them passing me the basketball."

A'ja's ferocious rise to the top hasn't been confined to the United States. Named to the US Olympic team in 2021 and 2024, she took her skills to the Tokyo and Paris Games. And she led her team to gold both times.

Competitive. Humble. Relentless. Efficient. Spirited. Authentic. Unstoppable. A'ja Wilson is many things. She's A'Rebel. She's A'Winner. She's A'Record Breaker. She's one of a kind. And that's just for starters.

"I DON'T THINK THERE IS A CEILING IN SIGHT FOR ME."

A'BEST SELLER

A'ja is proud of giving her all in every game. She's proud of the awards she's won, and she's honored to represent her country. But another accomplishment looms large. In 2024, A'ja published her book, ***Dear Black Girls: How to Be True to You***. She'd always dreamed of being an author. As someone with dyslexia, she never thought it would be possible. But like she did for all of the triumphs in her life, she got to work. She put pen to paper and shared her thoughts and experiences on the page. Meeting girls who have been moved by her words has brought her a whole new kind of joy.

TRAIN LIKE A'JA

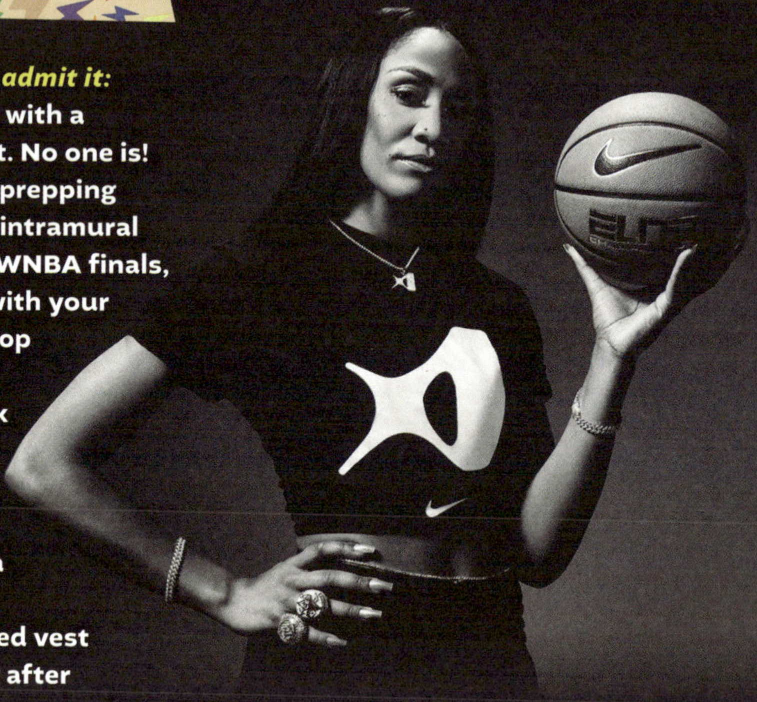

A'ja is the first to admit it: **She was not born with a perfect jump shot. No one is! Whether you are prepping for gym class, an intramural tournament, the WNBA finals, or an afternoon with your bestie and the hoop in your driveway, it takes hard work and dedication to get to the top of your game.**

As a teen, A'ja would strap on a 40-pound weighted vest and keep training after practice. In her career, she's spent countless hours perfecting her footwork, doing layup after layup, and pushing her endurance to the limit. Even if working out isn't your favorite thing (it's not A'ja's!), there are plenty of fun activities you can do to hone your skills. Here are a few you can do at home—some you can do without a basketball court or a hoop.

"WHEN IT COMES TO THE MINDSET OF WANTING TO GET BETTER AND WANTING TO BE GREAT AT SOMETHING OR EXECUTING SOMETHING— THAT'S WHAT I LIVE FOR."

Each of these exercises will require a little bit of space though, so take it to your backyard, a park, your driveway, your basement—anywhere you can move freely without the risk of breaking something if you drop the ball.

TWO HANDS!

There will be only one ball during a basketball game, but practicing with two balls will help you with your ball skills and coordination.

1. **Dribble two balls at the same time so they bounce in unison. Keep it up for 30 seconds.**
2. **Dribble two balls in an alternating pattern so they bounce one after the other. Keep it up for 30 seconds.**

BALL WRAPS

Basketball players are always on the move. So in this exercise, you will practice some ball handling while walking briskly from one point to another.

1. **Choose a starting point and an endpoint point (ideally 20–40 feet away, depending on how much space you have).**
2. **As you walk quickly from your starting point to your endpoint and back again, pass the ball from one hand to the next, circling it around your body. Try to keep the ball from touching your body as you move it. Repeat this step.**
3. **Reverse the direction you are passing the ball and complete two more laps back and forth.**

DRIBBLE, DRIBBLE, TAP

Basketball players are master dribblers. Here's a way to sharpen your dribbling skills!

1. **Choose a starting point and an endpoint (ideally 20–40 feet away, depending on how much space you have).**
2. **Crouch low and begin dribbling with your right hand. Keep your head up and your eyes forward. As you walk, dribble three times with your right hand, then tap the ground with your left. Continue this pattern until you reach your endpoint. Then turn around and repeat the exercise on your way back.**
3. **After you've completed two laps back and forth, switch hands and complete two more laps while dribbling the ball with your left hand and tapping the ground with your right.**

FIERCE FACT

A'ja doesn't use a lot of weights in her workouts. She prefers bodyweight workouts like lunges, squats, and clamshells.

"MY MAIN WORKOUT IS BASKETBALL PRACTICE. I GET MY EXERCISE IN ON THE COURT AND THEN IN THE WEIGHT ROOM."

SPIN AND SHOOT

If you have access to a hoop, here's a fun way to practice your footwork and your aim. Do this alone or with a partner.

1. **With your back to the basket, have a friend pass you the ball.**
2. **Catch it, then spin around, and shoot on the basket.**
3. **Try it 15 times, then swap places.**

If you are on your own, throw the ball away from yourself with a backspin so it bounces back toward you. Then catch the ball, spin around, and take a shot.

DEAR REBEL

Rebel Girls sat down with A'ja to discuss everything from hanging out with her grandmother and getting her first hoop to winning gold medals and the future of women in sports. And here is what she had to say.

Q. ***What advice do you have for girls who want to follow in your footsteps?***

A. Start at ground level. **It's okay to go at your own pace. It's okay to not be perfect at it on the first try.** I think when we look at the world today, everything looks so easy and so perfect and everyone makes it seem like it just happened like that. And no, absolutely not. **Fail, lose, cry, get embarrassed, and then do it all over again. Just wake up and do it all over again.** After a while, all those emotions are going to turn to success, winning, loving the game, passion—and now you're living your dream. Focus on the little things: your foundation, your footwork, your health, eating the right things, going to sleep. Those are the keys.

FIERCE FACT

A'ja wants girls to know that sports aren't always about the wins and losses and that your mindset can change your outlook. "If you lose a game," she says, just think, "So what? You're going to win tomorrow."

"GIVE ME A
CHALLENGE, AND
I PROMISE YOU
I'M GOING TO
TRY TO RUN
THROUGH A
BRICK WALL
TO GET
IT DONE."

"I LOVE MY JOB.
I PLAY WITH SO MUCH PASSION, AND I WANT PEOPLE TO FEEL THAT."

Q. ***What were you like as a child?***

A. I was **super shy**. I was a homebody. I loved my parents. It was just me and my mom and my dad growing up in the house, so they were my best friends. I was very curious about a lot of different things. **I loved being outside.** I didn't see people who looked like me, so I was like: *I'm the odd one out, so how do I fit in? Where can I go? Who can I turn to? Who can I talk to?* At a young age, **I spent a lot of time just figuring out what I want to do**, where I want to be in life. And I really connected with my grandmother. We got so tight and so close because we just stayed in the house and played games, watched shows, did little things. We probably did a lot of chores, but I was young, so I was just like, *I'm just* ***having fun with my grandma***. That was me. I was really low-key.

Q. ***How has basketball changed your life?***

A. It got me out of my shell. It allowed me to build bonds and relationships with people in a very unique way. I keep pretty much to myself in a lot of ways, but basketball allows me to bridge that gap to talk to people, learn their ways, see how they are, see what makes them go, what makes them happy, what makes them enjoy life—**not just basketball, but life**. It allows me to have conversations with people who I probably never would've gotten to if I didn't have a basketball in my hand. **I have to credit basketball for allowing me to be me.**

Q. ***Is it possible to be ultracompetitive and show good sportsmanship?***

A. Yeah. I pride myself on the fact that we're going to be competitors, and **I'm going to give it 100 percent**. But at the same time, when it's all said and done, we can go get food. **We can laugh it up and chop it up and know that it's just a game.** It's entertainment. Basketball doesn't define me, in the same way dyslexia doesn't define me. **My competitive spirit—I try to let it fuel me in a very positive way.**

Q. ***What would you say to girls who feel like they haven't found their thing yet?***

A. **That it's okay. I think sometimes we don't hear that enough.** In due time, you're going to get exactly what your niche is and you're going to understand why it took so long. You need to see it. **You need it to fail. You need to grow for you to really love something.** I think that the biggest thing is letting them know that it's okay, but it's going to come. **And when you see it, it's going to be clear as day.**

Q. ***What are your hopes for the future of basketball? For women in sports?***

A. That people respect us and **give us the respect that's been long overdue**. We work just as hard as anybody else, and we deserve to have a seat at the table and get our plate and eat just like everyone else. And it's coming. It's brewing. We see it every single day, but **we'll continue to lay that foundation down for women** to understand that we got a seat at the table as well. We're going to extend this seat, and we're going to bring chairs along with us.

"I'M HAVING FUN WITH IT AND LOVE WHAT I DO, BUT I STILL FEEL LIKE I HAVE SO MUCH TO GIVE."

YOU'RE UP!

Basketball makes A'ja feel confident and free. "When you get into your zone and everything is just flowing for you, and you're happy and confident and you can't wait to wake up the next morning and do that thing again? That's it. Your thing." She says, "Dive into it with everything you've got." What is your thing? How does it make you feel? (Remember: it's totally okay if it's not sports related or if there are a few things you love to do.)

I Love basketball when I at least just
dribble a ball it makes me feel amazing
I am going to work hard to get better
and achieve my dreams to the WNBA

As a kid, A'ja tried out many different sports and activities. Her father said she learned a lot from each sport she played. "Volleyball gave her excellent timing," he said, "and soccer gave great awareness of where her feet were without looking down." She also learned about teamwork, communication, discipline, and perseverance. What have you learned from the sports and activities you've tried?

I have learned that when I was in
2nd grade I did future girl soccer I
Loved the game but I learned
to focus because the coaches
were very hard on me so
I listened to them trying
not to get in trouble.

A'ja still gets nervous before every game. "Once the ball goes up, though," she says, "it's a different story. When the game starts, I'm locked in, and I'm ready to rock and roll." To battle stress and nerves, she sleeps in, prays, meditates, watches cartoons, and plays with her puppies. Before a game, she talks to her teammates. Sometimes they turn the music up, dance around, and sing out loud. What do you do to calm yourself when you are feeling stressed? Are there some new strategies you might like to try?

somtimes to deal with stress I just go up into my room so I dont put everyone in a bad mood thing I would like to try is tell somone I never really talk about my feelings with my parents

"I WANT TO ALLOW GIRLS TO SEE THE GAME FOR WHAT IT IS, WHICH IS A BEAUTIFUL **ART** AND FUN THING THAT WE DO."

Leadership means a lot to A'ja. She spends time thinking about how she can push her teammates to be their best and inspire others to name their goals and reach them. What can you do to inspire your loved ones to be their best selves?

my younger sister
e

When A'ja won her first gold medal in Tokyo, Japan, she took time to feel proud of her accomplishment. She also reflected on how far she'd come—from a shy little girl who didn't want to play basketball to an Olympian representing her country and winning on the world's biggest stage. Describe a moment in your life that makes you feel proud. How did you get there? What did it feel like?

FIERCE FACT

At the Tokyo Games, A'ja averaged 16.5 points and 7.3 rebounds per game. Three years later in Paris, she averaged 18.7 points and 10.2 rebounds per game.

A'ja likes to write down her goals and check them off. That way, she can see that she's getting the work done. What are your goals? Write them here. Visualize yourself reaching them. And when you're ready, add a big colorful check mark to show your awesome progress.

A’ja’s beloved grandmother always said to her, “The best is yet to come.” This phrase reminds her to stay positive and think of her bright future. “You may be in uncomfortable situations. You may be around a lot of thunderstorms, but just know that the sun is going to shine one day,” says A’ja. “There is something better out there if you continue to work hard.” What is a phrase or mantra that comforts you? In what way?

“THE MAIN GOAL FOR MYSELF IS JUST TO BE BETTER THAN I WAS LAST YEAR.”

TIME TO RHYME

Put your hands together and celebrate A'ja.

A'ja Wilson's on top top top—
Can't take her spot spot spot.

She's a real one through through through,
Always does what she'll do do do.

She won MVP-P-P.
1, 2, and 3 3 3.

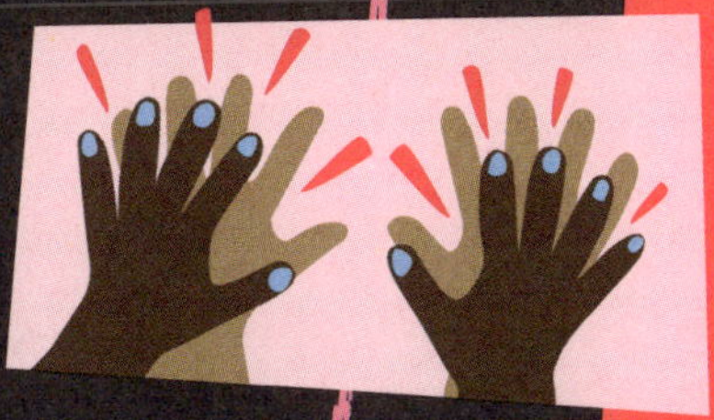

Her game is tea tea tea.
She made history-ree-ree.

From the mid, it's a wrap wrap wrap.
All buckets, no cap cap cap.

They said she wasn't enough nuff nuff.
So she did it for us us us.

And if you talk smack smack smack,
She's gonna clap back back back.

Her drip's elite-lite-lite.
It can't be beat beat beat.

She's A-One, it's clear clear clear,
Cuz A'ja's top tier tier tier!

A'ja Wilson's on top top top—
Can't take her spot spot spot.

** set to the tune of "Miss Mary Mack"*

SIGNATURE STYLE

A'ja is a legend on and off the court. She trains hard and dominates in competition. And she does it all with a distinctive style and energy. And now she has a signature shoe that spotlights her unstoppable flair: bold, versatile, and unapologetically real.

A'RECORD BREAKER
A'SHOT BLOCKER
A'WARRIOR
A'REBEL
A'ONE

"WHEN ATHLETES WEAR MY SHOE, I WANT THEM TO FEEL THE POWER BEHIND THAT LOGO: THE POWER TO DREAM BIG, THEN PUT IN THE WORK—IN STYLE AND CONFIDENCE."

TIME TO SHINE

"When I play, I hope to show with every emotion that I have that I love the game of basketball," says A'ja. And that's what she hopes for every one of you out there—that you find the thing that makes you feel self-assured and joyful and whole. Whether it is singing in a choir, learning computer programming, playing soccer, or shooting hoops, get out there and enjoy it. Don't waste time second-guessing yourself or worrying about what other people think about the things that make you shine.

Yes, there will be hard work. You will flub some high notes, mess up some code, and miss some free throws. And that is 100 percent okay, as long as you get out there and try again. Take advice from the legend herself: "If you believe in yourself and surround yourself with good people, the sky is the limit for you."

"I LOVE BASKETBALL. I LOVE THE GAME. IT BRINGS ME SO MUCH JOY."

#22

MORE BOOKS!

For more inspiring stories about amazing women and girls, and to get tried-and-tested advice on growing up and pursuing your dreams, check out other Rebel Girls books.

SCAN FOR MORE!

For more stories about game-changing women and girls, scan here!

ABOUT REBEL GIRLS

Rebel Girls, a certified B Corporation, is a global, multi-platform empowerment brand dedicated to helping raise the most inspired and confident generation of girls. The brand purposefully creates content, products, and experiences to empower Generation Alpha girls and equip them with the knowledge and tools they need to thrive. Because confident girls will radically transform the world.

With a growing community of 38 million self-identified Rebel Girls spanning more than 115 countries, the brand engages with Gen Alpha through its book series, premier app, events, and merchandise. To date, Rebel Girls has sold more than 11 million books in 62 languages and reached 75 million digital listens/views. Award recognition includes the *New York Times* bestseller list, 2022 Apple Design Award for Social Impact, 10 Webby Awards, and more.

REBEL GiRLS SPORT is a bold new destination for tween and teen girls to inspire, build confidence, celebrate women athletes, and spark lifelong fandom through content, experiences, and products.

JOiN THE REBEL GiRLS COMMUNiTY

Head to rebelgirls.com and join our email list for exclusive sneak peeks, new content drops, creative activities, and more. If you want to say hi or have any questions, email us at **hello@rebelgirls.com**. We love hearing from you.

MORE PLACES TO FiND US!

Watch: youtube.com/RebelGirls **Listen: rebelgirls.com/audio**

Shop: rebelgirls.com/shop

And for your daily dose of Rebel Girls, be sure to follow us on Instagram & Facebook **@rebelgirls**